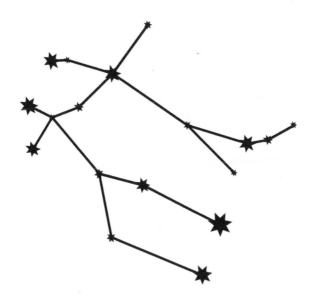

 ONE IDEA PRESS

Ordering Information:
Quantity sales. Special discounts are available on quantity purchases by
corporations, associations, and others. For details, contact the "Special Sales
Department" at the following email address: hello@oneideapress.com.

Paperback Edition: 978-1-944134-45-7
Hardback Edition: 978-1-944134-46-4

Printed in the United States of America

Gemini

a love letter

Heidi Rose Robbins

with illustrations by
Wyoh Lee

hello love.

(yes, you)

Friends,

I'm so glad you are holding this book! It is filled
with encouragement and an ongoing invitation
for us all to be more fully who we are.

The best way to work with these books is to
purchase one for each of your signs — your
Sun, Moon, and Rising Sign.

These are the three most important po-
sitions in your astrological chart. You can
discover what these are if you enter your
exact time, date, and place of birth in any
online astrology site. Each position has something unique to offer.

When you read the book for your Moon, think
of it as an energy that is very available
to you. It's a place where you might feel
comfortable. The Moon has to do with our

emotional life, our patterns of behavior, and circumstances of our childhood. We can rely on the Moon, but we also want to work to shed the patterns that no longer serve us.

The Sun is our present personality. We can learn a lot about our everyday self in the world. We can learn about the energies we have readily available to us to use in service to our highest calling.

The Rising Sign is the most important point. It is the sign that was rising as we took our first breath. It holds the key to our soul's calling. It is an energy we want to cultivate and be generous with throughout our lives.

So — enjoy the journey. Be sure to read them all!

Welcome
{13}

My dear Gemini,

This little book is a love letter to your lively, curious self. It is written to remind you of your many gifts. It is written to be a loving mirror so any page can remind you who you truly are. Take it in, dear Gemini. Don't read too quickly. I know how you like to keep things moving and interesting! But promise me you'll slow down enough to see your brilliant and vital self in these pages.

This little book will also explore those places in ourselves that start to close when we want to open, the part of us that hesitates when we want to act. We all have our quirks and difficulties, after all. But if we return again and again to our vitality, vulnerability, and sense of possibility, we can outgrow our closures one by one.

Think of this book as a treasure chest containing the golden coins of YOU. Open it when you wish to remember your beauty, worth or great potential. And remember, too, this Gemini part of you is just one voice in the symphony of YOU. It cannot possibly contain your complexity and bounty. But it can begin to name just a few of your gifts.

Read this out loud when you can. Read this in the morning. Read it before bed. Read it when you need encouragement. Let it fuel your curiosity and wonder. But READ IT. And own it! And use it! And claim it! This is your love letter, Gemini. This is the song of YOU.

Big love,
Heidi Rose

Celebrating Gemini

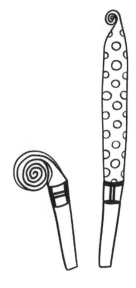

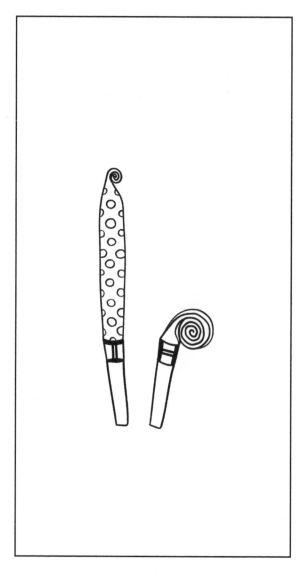

As you read this celebration, you will sometimes say "Yes, yes, yes! This is me!" And you may likewise sometimes feel that you have not yet lived into some of these qualities. This is honoring and celebrating the very best of your Gemini energy. This is naming the full, conscious, awakened use of your Gemini gifts. We are sounding the note of THE POSSIBLE. So, even if you feel you still have work to do in certain areas — as do we all — let these words be inspiration to offer your best Self!

♊

You are a messenger.

You get the word out, dear Gemini. You sound the call. You write, speak, interview and converse. You love to share information quickly. You reach out, call, email, and send snail-mail. You are a distributor of the good word.

♊

You build bridges.

You, dear Gemini, build bridges of light and connection so we can spread a little more goodwill. You know how to bridge the opposites, to invite two very different perspectives into the same room to find common ground. You get the conversation started that leads to greater understanding.

Ⅱ

You are insatiably curious.

You have all the questions,
Gemini. You never run out. You
could write entire books filled
with questions. You like to ask
them and you like to answer
them. Your questions only lead to
more questions! And your questions
spark the curiosity of others. The
discovery never ends.

♊

You are young at heart.

You embody childlike wonder, Gemini. You are quick, clever, buoyant, and youthful. You never stop looking at the world through the lens of curiosity and innocence. This is a great gift. You will never get bored or jaded. You are an inspiration.

Ⅱ

You are a fact finder.

Isn't it delicious to collect all
the facts? You are smart!
And you know how to get the
information you need. You are
willing to read, research, and
investigate to discover the
information required. And you
always have those facts at the
tip of your tongue. You are the
fact repository!

♊

You are a multi-tasker.

No one can keep as many things going at once as you can, sweet Gemini. You have 10 pots on the stove and ten irons in the fire. Sometimes you have a phone in your hand, a pen in the other, and a headset connected to the computer all at work at once! How do you do it?

♊

You are delightfully flirty.

Everyone is interesting! And you
also have the rare gift of making
people feel interesting. You love to
work a room and light people up as
you go. Your vivacious energy fills
a gathering. And you leave people
feeling lighter and loved.

Ⅱ

You are smart.

It's as simple as that, dear
Gemini. You are a thinker. And
a reader. And often a writer.
You want to know. You educate
yourself. You get even smarter
by engaging with others, sharing
ideas and then investigating
something new.

Ⅱ

You are quick.

It's hard to keep up with you,
Gemini! Your sign is one
of great and constant movement.
You are on the go. You don't
rest long anywhere. There is so
much to see and do. You alight
like a butterfly and then are on
your way.

♊

You are a connector.

You love to relate, dear Gemini.
And you love to connect others so
they can relate too! You instigate
conversations between those
that would benefit. You make
introductions. You even connect
ideas. You marry two streams
of thought and come up with a
whole new way of thinking about
the subject.

♊

You love to teach and
you love to learn.

You are always willing to share
what you know. You love best to
exchange information. You are
ever the eager student and ever
the willing teacher or facilitator.
You are a true educator. And
your childlike wonder will always
welcome new information.

Ⅱ

You light up a room.

You are a bright light moving at lightning speed engaging all you meet. When we hear a peal of laughter in the corner, there is sure to be a Gemini present delighting all in her midst. You don't land anywhere long, but you spark light wherever you go.

♊

You are a lover of language and gifted with words.

Many of you, dear Gemini, are amazing writers. You love language and love to share it. Some of you are public speakers and others love the dance with the page. You have a way with words. Sometimes you are playful with language and sometimes powerful. But you certainly know how to communicate.

Ⅱ

You can talk with anyone about anything.

When your curiosity marries your love of relating, it's clear that you can strike up a conversation with almost anyone! You are not afraid to engage and you have a myriad of topics to discuss at any given moment. You happily engage with any willing soul.

♊

You embody the spirit of goodwill

Your true gift is how you offer
your loving wisdom, Gemini. You
marry the head to the heart.
And when you connect, you do so
with love and decency.
You leave people better than
you found them.

Ⅱ

You are versatile.

You are never stuck in an old
pattern. Dear Gemini, you are
always willing to change it up. You
don't get stuck easily. You are
mutable, changeable and ever
evolving. You are flexible in how
you think about things.

Ⅱ

You are gregarious.

What fun is it being alone when
there are so many magnificent
humans with whom to connect?
You have so many questions and
curiosities that of course you
want to be out and amongst
the public. Who knows whom you
might meet!

♊

You are a true
conversationalist.

You are brilliant at asking
questions that are evocative and
interesting. You want to know. You
want to share what you know. Any
conversation with you will be lively!
And you spark group conversations
as well, not just one on one. You get
everyone involved. A once silent
room is no longer once you've done
your work.

♊

You know how to debate.

You've got all the words. You
know how to argue. Your facility
with language makes it difficult
for anyone to match your speed
and intelligence. You are facile
with facts. We all want you on
our team!

♊

You are lively, spontaneous and witty.

And charming, smart, light and full of banter, dear Gemini. You amuse and delight anyone in your midst. You tell funny stories. You offer information that is inspiring. You keep the crowd laughing and on their toes!

Living Your Gemini Love

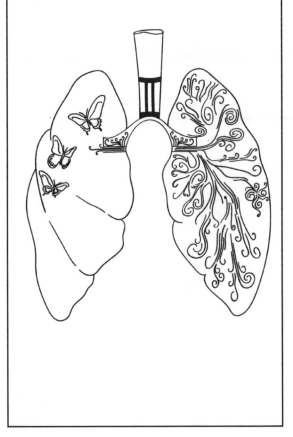

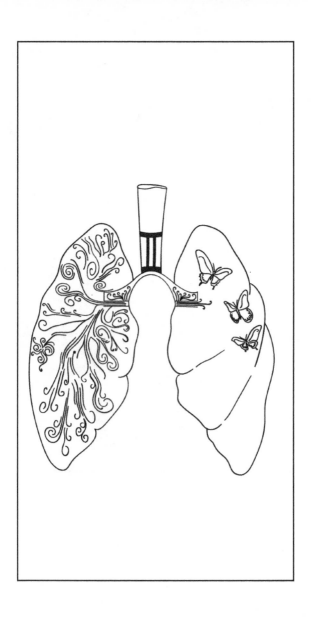

How are you feeling, dear Gemini? Can you sense the potency of your gifts? Do you want to make the very most of this spirited, intelligent energy of Gemini? Here are some thoughts about how to live fully into your Gemini love and how to nourish your Gemini spirit. Consider them little whispered reminders meant to help you THRIVE. Consider them 'action items' — a loving Gemini "to-do" list. Consider them invitations to live your loving intelligence.

♊

Cultivate Conversation with Your Soul.

Have an ongoing conversation with the true YOU. You might ask yourself a question and journal the answer. You might ask your soul self questions and sit in contemplation to see what emerges. Refuse superficiality. Let your Soul self — your best self — infuse your daily exchanges. Listen to the loving, wise YOU within and when you are ready, offer it up without.

♊

Spend a day in bed with
a good book.

Nourish yourself with your love
of words. Every now and then
disappear with a new book and
dive into the dialogue between
you and the page.

♊

Organize a conference or community event.

You are a connector, facilitator and networker. You can organize a gathering with lightning speed. Invest in anything that will educate Humanity or grow our goodwill toward one another. Be a builder of bridges in your community.

♊

Write what you think.

Get your thoughts on the page.
Journal. Write an essay. Write a
letter. Write a letter to the local
paper. Leave a comment. Be the
messenger for what you believe
in. Communicate in all the ways
you know how. Try doing them all
at once in Gemini fashion.

♊

Interview someone you admire.

You know how to ask the questions that get the best out of anyone. Ask them all. Uncover the story of another someone. Share what you love about someone by helping them get their message out. Be the incredible reporter you are.

♊

Create little outings and adventures for yourself.

You love a good day-long adventure. You don't need to travel far and wide all the time. You love a good trip to a nearby little town you've never explored. Find a new place to eat. Drive to a local farm and pick apples. Search out interesting activities!

♊

Work with Children.

You have the awe, wonder, and curiosity of a child. You are wide-open and eager. This gives you such an IN with actual kids. You understand a child's need to know. You understand how easy it is to get bored and need something NEW. Teach kids. Talk with kids. Hang out with them. They will LOVE you.

Ⅱ

Promote loving relationship.

Can you, dear Gemini, feel how
your heart is connected to every
heart in this Solar System? As
we evolve the Gemini energy, we
begin to realize we are capable
of igniting a chain of fiery love.
You are great at making these
connections and building bridges
of kindness. We need you!

Growing Your Gemini Love

Sometimes, dear Gemini, we swing too far in one direction and need to invite a balancing energy to set us right. We are all growing and need to address the parts of ourselves that have not developed as fully. The opportunity for Gemini is to invite Sagittarius (your opposite sign) into the picture. Here are ways to grow your Gemini love to be more focused, visionary and encouraging.

♊

Practice the power of focus.

Yes, you are a multi-tasker
but you will always benefit by
strengthening your focus muscles.
Sometimes you have to choose
and commit. It will feel enormously
satisfying to follow one true path
for awhile and not allow yourself
to get distracted. Name your big
vision and keep your eye on that.

Ⅱ

Harness restlessness.

Notice the ways you disperse
your energy. Notice all the
unnecessary activities that
diminish your power, dear Gemini.
Try to sit in stillness and choose
the next achievable goal —
however small. Sometimes, too,
vigorous physical activity will help
calm the nervous system.

♊

Go deeper.

You love and are curious about so many things. But to grow you must occasionally choose one and go deeper. Go beneath the surface. Investigate. Penetrate. Be tenacious. Come to a deeper understanding of whatever it is you choose to study. And even in conversation, dive below the surface. Ask the questions that lead to truth.

Ⅱ

Quiet the mind.

It's easy to think about thinking.
And then think about that.
What helps you drop out of the
spin of the mind into the quiet
of the body or the intelligence
of the heart? Find the practices
that slow down the mind
and the talk. Choose to say
less. Experiment with silence
and stillness.

♊

Don't get lost in the multitude of possibilities.

When you can, think BIG PICTURE. You love a lot of things, dear Gemini. But occasionally ask, "What really speaks to me at this particular moment?" And give yourself wholeheartedly to it. Overwhelm creates an inability to do any one thing. Choose the one thing that is lighting you up right now.

Ⅱ

Remember to infuse your
intelligence with love.
Move beyond dry facts.

Dry facts are dry. True wisdom
comes when we can marry the
mind with the heart. We strive
to have a loving mind and an
intelligent heart. The dry fact
is only that unless supported by
compassion and sensitivity. Ask
yourself, "Why do we want or need
to know this?" Share what
is meaningful.

♊

Breathe More Deeply.

Gemini rules the lungs. And you, dear Gemini, might tend to breathe more shallowly. Practice taking deep breaths whenever you think of it. It will help every part of you feel quieter and more calm.

Questions to Inspire Sharing Your Gemini Love

Dear Gemini, here are a few prompts and questions that might inspire or clarify your mission. Grab your journal. Write for 15 minutes about each. Read your answers out loud to a friend. Read them out loud for yourself. Let this exploration nourish your Gemini curiosity and desire to share.

♊

What am I a messenger
for in the world?

♊

If I were going to write
3 books in my life,
what would the titles be?

What would they be about?

♊

What am I
deeply curious about?

Make a list!

♊

What are my
big questions?

Ⅱ

Write this:
I love...
I don't love...

♊

What are some things
I don't know yet?

Ⅱ

Who would I love
to talk to and about what?

♊

When I scatter my energy,
it looks like this...

♊

Where do I feel split
in myself?

Ⅱ

Where can I dig a
little deeper?

Ⅱ

If I listen deeply,
I hear this...